WISE SAYINGS

of

JESUS

LION

Compiled by Kate Kirkpatrick
This edition copyright © 2011 Lion Hudson
The author asserts the moral right
to be identified as the author of this work

A Lion Book
an imprint of
Lion Hudson plc
Wilkinson House, Jordan Hill Road,
Oxford OX2 8DR, England
www.lionhudson.com
ISBN 978 0 7459 5533 9

Distributed by:
UK: Marston Book Services, PO Box 269,
Abingdon, Oxon, OX14 4YN
USA: Trafalgar Square Publishing, 814 N.
Franklin Street, Chicago, IL 60610
USA Christian Market: Kregel Publications,
PO Box 2607, Grand Rapids, MI 49501
First edition 2011
10 9 8 7 6 5 4 3 2 1 0
All rights reserved

Acknowledgments

pp. 6, 52, 59: Scripture quotations are
from *The Holy Bible, English Standard Version*,
published by HarperCollins Publishers,
copyright © 2001 Crossway Bibles, a division
of Good News Publishers. Used by permission.
All rights reserved. pp. 23, 33, 42: Extracts
from the *Authorized Version of the Bible* (*The King
James Bible*), the rights in which are vested in
the Crown, are reproduced by permission of
the Crown's Patentee, Cambridge University
Press. pp. 12, 18–19, 36, 38, 43, 44–45,
54, 55, 58: Scripture taken from the NEW
AMERICAN STANDARD BIBLE®, Copyright
© 1960,1962,1963,1968,1971,1972,1973,1
975,1977,1995 by The Lockman Foundation.
Used by permission. pp. 7, 10, 11, 14, 16,
24–25, 26, 27, 28, 34, 37, 39, 46–47, 56:
Scripture quotations taken from the *Holy Bible,
New International Version*, copyright © 1973,
1978, 1984 International Bible Society. Used
by permission of Zondervan and Hodder
& Stoughton Limited. All rights reserved.
The 'NIV' and 'New International Version'
trademarks are registered in the United States

Patent and Trademark Office by International
Bible Society. Use of either trademark
requires the permission of International Bible
Society. UK trademark number 1448790. pp.
35, 57: Taken from the *New Jerusalem Bible*,
published and copyright © 1985 by Darton,
Longman and Todd Ltd and les Editions du
Cerf, and by Doubleday, a division of Bantam
Doubleday Dell Publishing Group, Inc.
Used by permission of Darton, Longman
and Todd Ltd, and Doubleday, a division of
Random House, Inc. p. 49: *The New King James
Version* copyright © 1982, 1979 by Thomas
Nelson, Inc. J.B. Phillips Reprinted with the
permission of Simon & Schuster from *The
New Testament in Modern English, Revised Edition*,
translated by J. B. Phillips. Copyright © 1958,
1960, 1972 by J. B. Phillips. Reprinted from
*The New Testament in Modern English, Revised
Edition*, translated by J.B. Phillips. Published
by HarperCollins Publishers Ltd. pp. 13,
22: Scripture quotations are taken from the
Holy Bible, New Living Translation, copyright ©
1996. Used by permission of Tyndale House
Publishers, Inc., Wheaton, Illinois 60189. All
rights reserved. pp. 32: Scripture quotations
are from the *Revised Standard Version* published
by HarperCollins Publishers, copyright ©
1989 by the Division of Christian Education
of the National Council of the Churches of
Christ in the USA, and are used by permission.
All rights reserved. pp. 17, 52: Scripture
quotations are from the *New Revised Standard
Version* published by HarperCollins Publishers,
copyright © 1989 by the Division of Christian
Education of the National Council of the
Churches of Christ in the USA, and are used
by permission. All rights reserved.

A catalogue record for this book is available
from the British Library
Typeset in 10.5/12 Perpetua and 10/24
Zapfino
Printed and bound in China

ONTENTS

INTRODUCTION

Of all the world's great spiritual teachers, none has had a more profound influence than Jesus Christ. His wisdom and teachings of kindness astonished his first audiences – "No one ever spoke like this man," said the Temple guards (John 7:46) – and they have inspired countless generations since.

This book brings together some of his most insightful stories and sayings, as recorded in the four Gospels. Despite the passing of 2,000 years, they are still as pertinent and applicable today as they were when first spoken.

*Heaven and earth will pass away,
but my words will never pass away.*

LUKE 21:33

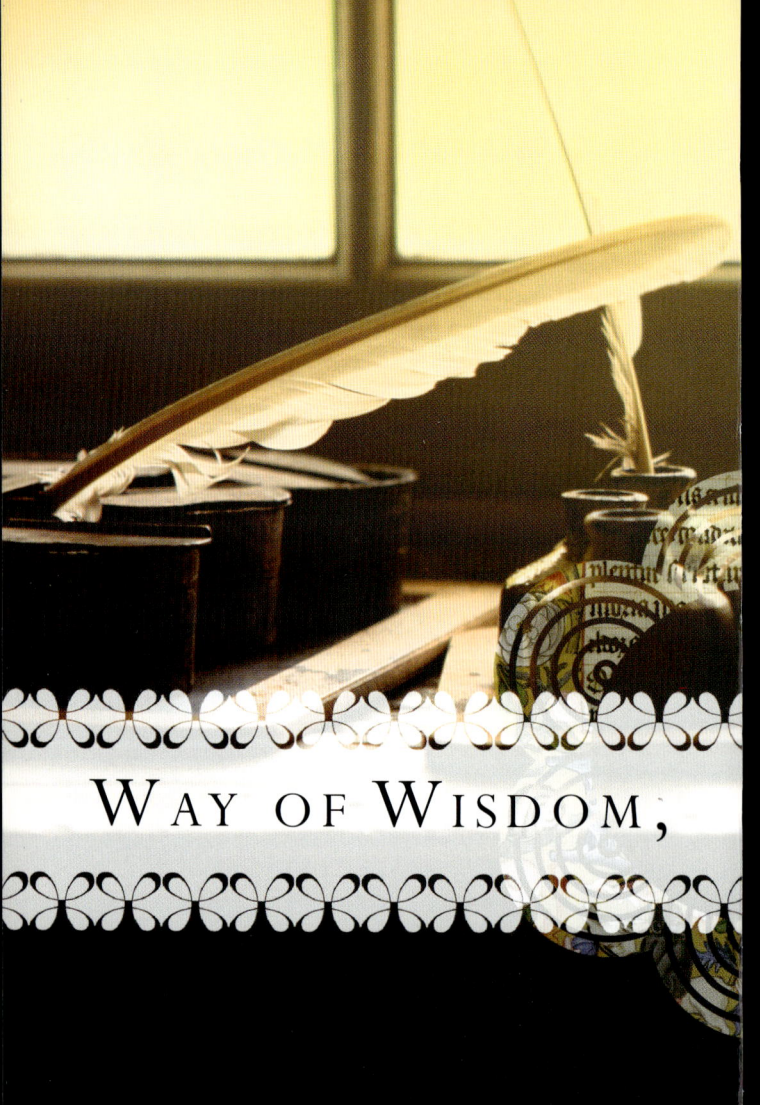

WAY OF WISDOM,

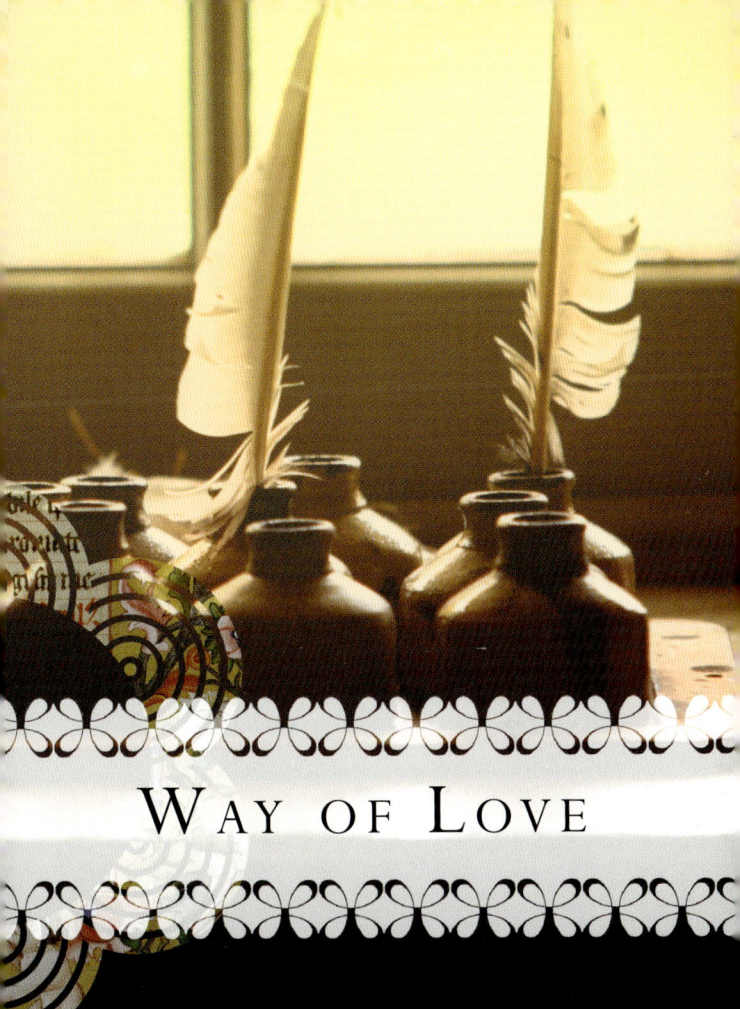

WAY OF LOVE

My command
is this: Love
each other as I
have loved you.

JOHN 15:12

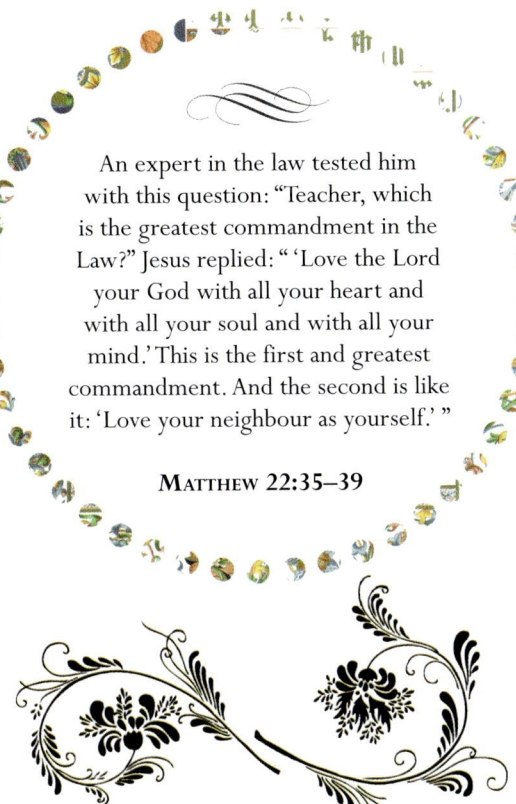

An expert in the law tested him with this question: "Teacher, which is the greatest commandment in the Law?" Jesus replied: " 'Love the Lord your God with all your heart and with all your soul and with all your mind.' This is the first and greatest commandment. And the second is like it: 'Love your neighbour as yourself.' "

MATTHEW 22:35–39

o not judge, and you will not be judged; and do not condemn, and you will not be condemned; pardon, and you will be pardoned. Give, and it will be given to you. They will pour into your lap a good measure – pressed down, shaken together, and running over. For by your standard of measure it will be measured to you in return.

Why do you look at the speck that is in your brother's eye, but do not notice the log that is in your own eye? Or how can you say to your brother, "Brother, let me take out the speck that is in your eye," when you yourself do not see the log that is in your own eye? You hypocrite, first take the log out of your own eye, and then you will see clearly to take out the speck that is in your brother's eye.

LUKE 6:37–38, 41–42

Let the one who has

never sinned throw the

first stone!

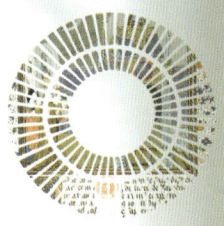

As the Father has loved me, so have I loved you. Now remain in my love. If you obey my commands, you will remain in my love, just as I have obeyed my Father's commands and remain in his love. I have told you this so that my joy may be in you and that your joy may be complete. My command is this: Love each other as I have loved you. Greater love has no one than this, that he lay down his life for his friends. You are my friends if you do what I command. I no longer call you servants, because a servant does not know his master's business. Instead, I have called you friends, for everything that I learned from my Father I have made known to you. You did not choose me, but I chose you and appointed you to go and bear fruit – fruit that will last. Then the Father will give you whatever you ask in my name. This is my command: Love each other.

JOHN 15:9–17

remain in
my love

Love your enemies, do good to those who hate you, bless those who curse you, pray for those who mistreat you. If someone strikes you on one cheek, turn to him the other also. If someone takes your cloak, do not stop him from taking your tunic. Give to everyone who asks you, and if anyone takes what belongs to you, do not demand it back. Do to others as you would have them do to you.

LUKE 6:27–31

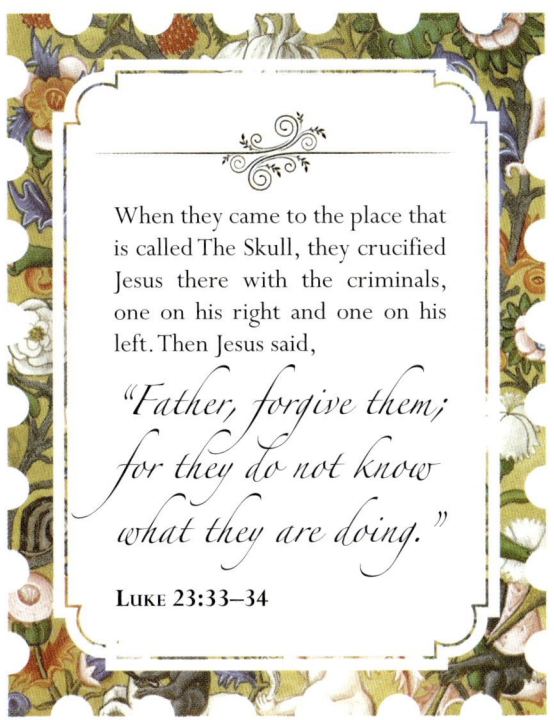

When they came to the place that is called The Skull, they crucified Jesus there with the criminals, one on his right and one on his left. Then Jesus said,

"Father, forgive them; for they do not know what they are doing."

LUKE 23:33–34

"A man was going down from Jerusalem to Jericho, and fell among robbers, and they stripped him and beat him, and went away leaving him half dead. And by chance a priest was going down on that road, and when he saw him, he passed by on the other side. Likewise a Levite also, when he came to the place and saw him, passed by on the other side. But a Samaritan, who was on a journey, came upon him; and when he saw him, he felt compassion, and came to him and bandaged up his wounds, pouring oil and wine on them; and he put him on his own beast, and brought him to an inn and took care of him.

"On the next day he took out two denarii and gave them to the innkeeper and said, 'Take care of him; and whatever more you spend, when I return I will repay you.'

"Which of these three do you think proved to be a neighbour to the man who fell into the robbers' hands?"

And he said, "The one who showed mercy toward him." Then Jesus said to him,

"Go and do the same."

LUKE 10:30–37

HIS EYE IS ON

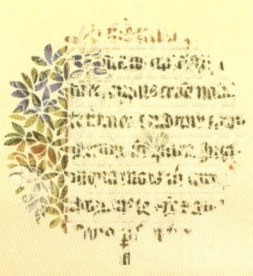

THE SPARROW

What is the price of two sparrows –
one copper coin? But not a single
sparrow can fall to the ground
without your Father knowing it.

Matthew 10:29

Come unto me,
all ye that labour
and are heavy
laden, and I will
give you rest.

MATTHEW 11:28

Therefore I tell you, do not worry about your life, what you will eat or drink; or about your body, what you will wear. Is not life more important than food, and the body more important than clothes? Look at the birds of the air; they do not sow or reap or store away in barns, and yet your heavenly Father feeds them. Are you not much more valuable than they? Who of you by worrying can add a single hour to his life?

And why do you worry about clothes? See how the lilies of the field grow. They do not labour or spin. Yet I tell you that not even Solomon in all his splendour was dressed like one of these. If that is how God clothes the grass of the field, which is here today and tomorrow is thrown into the fire, will he not much more clothe you, O you of little faith? So do not worry, saying, "What shall we eat?" or "What shall we drink?" or "What shall we wear?" For the pagans run after all these things, and your heavenly Father knows that you need them.

*But seek first his kingdom
and his righteousness, and
all these things will be given
to you as well.*

Therefore do not worry about tomorrow, for
tomorrow will worry about itself. Each day
has enough trouble of its own.

MATTHEW 6:25–34

Peace I leave with you; my peace I give you. I do not give to you as the world gives. Do not let your hearts be troubled and do not be afraid. … The world must learn that I love the Father and that I do exactly what my Father has commanded me.

JOHN 14:27, 31

The devil said to him, "If you are the Son of God, tell this stone to become bread." Jesus answered, "It is written: 'Man does not live on bread alone.'"

Luke 4:3–4

I have told you these things, so that in me you may have peace. In this world you will have trouble. But take heart! I have overcome the world.

JOHN 16:33

have peace

WHERE YOUR

TREASURE IS

*For where your
treasure is, there
will your heart
be also.*

MATTHEW 6:21

What shall it profit a man, if
he shall gain the whole world,
and lose his own soul?

MARK 8:36

e told them this parable: "The ground of a certain rich man produced a good crop. He thought to himself, 'What shall I do? I have no place to store my crops.' Then he said, 'This is what I'll do. I will tear down my barns and build bigger ones, and there I will store all my grain and my goods. And I'll say to myself, "You have plenty of good things laid up for many years. Take life easy; eat, drink and be merry."' But God said to him, 'You fool! This very night your life will be demanded from you. Then who will get what you have prepared for yourself?'"

LUKE 12:16–20

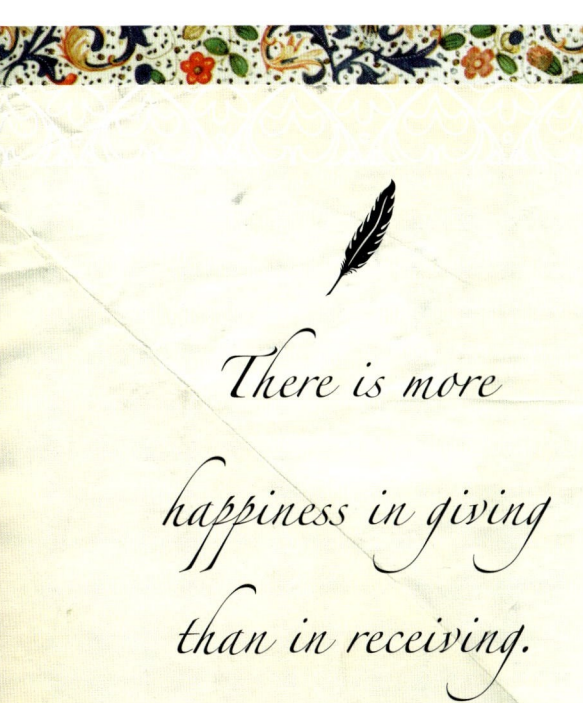

There is more

happiness in giving

than in receiving.

Acts 20:35

He who is faithful in a very little thing is faithful also in much; and he who is unrighteous in a very little thing is unrighteous also in much.

Luke 16:10

When you give to the needy, do not let your left hand know what your right hand is doing, so that your giving may be in secret. Then your Father, who sees what is done in secret, will reward you.

MATTHEW 6:3–4

"Beware, and be on your guard against every form of greed; for not even when one has an abundance does his life consist of his possessions."

Luke 12:15

For whoever exalts himself will
be humbled, and whoever humbles
himself will be exalted.

Matthew 23:12

LIGHT OF

THE WORLD

Ye are the light of the world. A city that is set on an hill cannot be hid. Neither do men light a candle, and put it under a bushel, but on a candlestick; and it giveth light unto all that are in the house. Let your light so shine before men, that they may see your good works, and glorify your Father which is in heaven.

MATTHEW 5:14–16

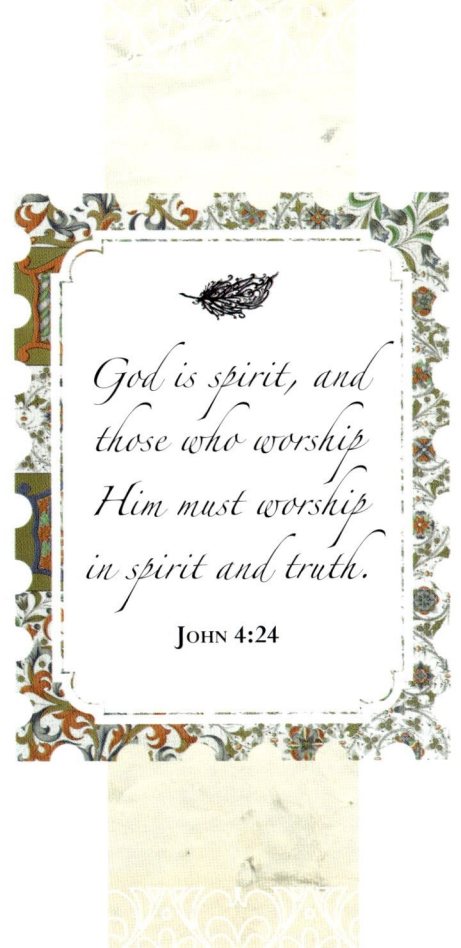

God is spirit, and those who worship Him must worship in spirit and truth.

JOHN 4:24

I am the vine, you are the branches; he who abides in Me and I in him, he bears much fruit, for apart from Me you can do nothing. If anyone does not abide in Me, he is thrown away as a branch and dries up; and they gather them, and cast them into the fire and they are burned. If you abide in Me, and My words abide in you, ask whatever you wish, and it will be done for you. My Father is glorified by this, that you bear much fruit, and so prove to be My disciples.

Just as the Father has loved Me, I have also loved you; abide in My love. If you keep My commandments, you will abide in My love; just as I have kept My Father's commandments and abide in His love. These things I have spoken to you so that My joy may be in you, and that your joy may be made full.

JOHN 15:5–11

Blessed are the poor in spirit,
for theirs is the kingdom of heaven.

Blessed are those who mourn,
for they will be comforted.

Blessed are the meek,
for they will inherit the earth.

Blessed are those who hunger and
thirst for righteousness,
for they will be filled.

Blessed are the merciful,
for they will be shown mercy.

Blessed are the pure in heart,
for they will see God.

Blessed are the peacemakers,
for they will be called sons of God.

Blessed are those who are persecuted
because of righteousness,
for theirs is the kingdom of heaven.

MATTHEW 5:3–12

A sower went out to sow. And it happened, as he sowed, that some seed fell by the wayside; and the birds of the air came and devoured it. Some fell on stony ground, where it did not have much earth; and immediately it sprang up because it had no depth of earth. But when the sun was up it was scorched, and because it had no root it withered away. And some seed fell among thorns; and the thorns grew up and chocked it, and it yielded no crop. But other seed fell on ground and yielded a crop that sprang up, increased and produced: some thirtyfold, some sixty, and some a hundred…. He who has ears to hear, let him hear!

MARK 4:3–9

let him hear

ASK AND YOU

WILL RECEIVE

Whatever you ask for in prayer,

believe that you have received it,

and it will be yours.

Mark 11:24

nd I tell you, ask, and it will be given to you; seek, and you will find; knock, and it will be opened to you. For everyone who asks receives, and the one who seeks finds, and to the one who knocks it will be opened. What father among you, if his son asks for a fish, will instead of a fish give him a serpent; or if he asks for an egg, will give him a scorpion? If you then, who are evil, know how to give good gifts to your children, how much more will the heavenly Father give the Holy Spirit to those who ask him!

LUKE 11:9–13

Come to Me, all who are weary and heavy-laden, and I will give you rest. Take My yoke upon you and learn from Me, for I am gentle and humble in heart, and you will find rest for your souls. For My yoke is easy and My burden is light.

MATTHEW 11:28–30

And the Lord said, "If you had faith like a mustard seed, you would say to this mulberry tree, 'Be uprooted and be planted in the sea'; and it would obey you."

LUKE 17:6

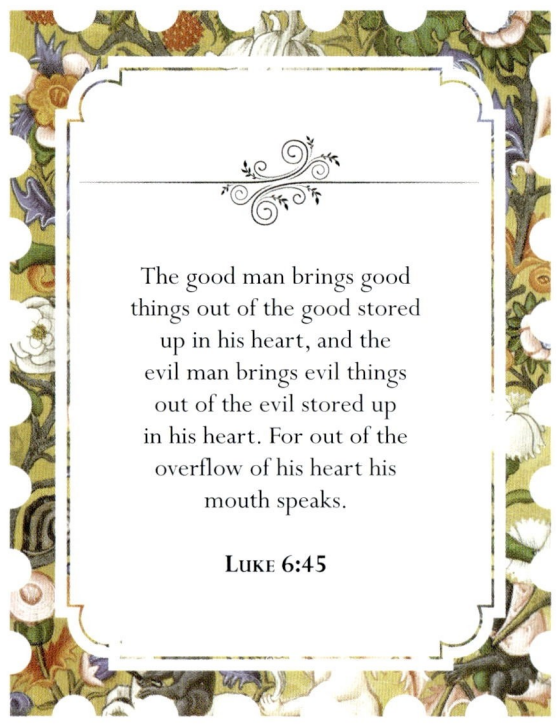

The good man brings good things out of the good stored up in his heart, and the evil man brings evil things out of the evil stored up in his heart. For out of the overflow of his heart his mouth speaks.

LUKE 6:45

Jesus said: "I am the Way; I am Truth and Life. No one can come to the Father except through me. If you know me, you will know my Father too. From this moment you know him and have seen him."

Philip said, "Lord, show us the Father and then we shall be satisfied."

Jesus said to him, "Have I been with you all this time, Philip, and you still do not know me?

Anyone who has seen me has seen the Father."

JOHN 14:6–9

The things that are
impossible with people are
possible with God.

LUKE 18:27

By this all people will
know that you are my
disciples, if you have love
for one another.

JOHN 13:35

ACKNOWLEDGMENTS

BACKGROUNDS:
iStock: Jussi Santaniemi

ILLUMINATED MANUSCRIPTS:
Alamy: Classic Image
Corbis: Fine Art Photographic Library; The Gallery Collection

MOTIFS:
iStock: Jamie Farrant; Oleksii Popovskyi; Pleio; Ryan Burke

PHOTOGRAPHS:
Corbis: pp. 8–9 Kazuhisa Natori/amanaimages; pp. 18, 39, 58 Image Source; pp. 19, 14–15, 59 Michele Constantini/ZenShui; pp. 14–15 Tom Grill; p. 45 Lucas Allen
iStock: pp. 6–7 Brue; pp. 20–21, 26–27, 49, 54-55 DNY59; p. 25 Steven Perry; p. 29 Werner Münzker; pp. 30–31 Carmen Martínez Banús; pp. 36–37 Esolla; pp. 40–41 Slavenko Vukasovic; pp. 46–47 Simon Howden; p. 50–51 Daniel Schweinert

COVER
Background: Jussi Santoniemi/iStock
Illuminated manuscript: The Gallery Collection/Corbis
Photograph: DNY59/iStock